HOW TO
UNCHAIN
YOUR BRAIN

In a hyperconnected multitasking world
Theo Compernolle

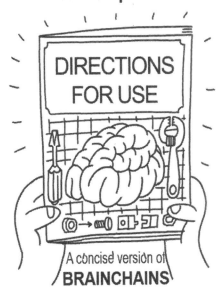

DIRECTIONS
FOR USE

A concise version of
BRAINCHAINS

A few of the comments about BrainChains

★★★★☆ on Amazon.com

★★★★★ on Amazon.co.uk

★★★★☆ on Amazon.cn

Stunning work, aggregating the best and newest research to create a User Manual for Your Brain! Whether all the new tech is leveraged as a positive tool or allowed to seduce us into numb- and dumbness is a fine line, and Theo delineates that with brilliance. Read at your peril.

David Allen

Excellent book on productivity. If you have read David Allen's Getting Things Done this book will be beneficial to comprehend the whole system and why we do what we do. Theo Compernolle's work is based on scientific research and backs up his arguments in style. If there is one thing you should take from BrainChains "Do not use your phone while driving" :-)

Addo General Mrch

I'm so glad I got my hands on this book. Forget all the other business books, tips and theories which everybody else uses, THIS is the book that will separate you away from the herd and should be read before anything else. This book will be kept on my desk instead of my bookshelf, as a constant reminder.

NoName

In a few words: an amazing book. Loved reading it. The author knows very well how to explain this matter in an open end very comprehensible way. I look at my laptop in a different way now. Must read!

4bozzza

This is one of those books that do have impact on your habits ... at least for me it did and that is I think the biggest value a book can have...

Joanne

... an easy to read "page turner"... which I feel everyone in the "connected" world should read.

Dave Scott, President

Top experience. Extended documentation.Accessible reading of "scientific" topics. Really professional. Appreciate the style and art of communication of the author. Congratulations. Excellent buy and investment.

Jean-Paul Antonus

"... a compelling, meticulously researched, and cleverly illustrated case against the twin tyrannies of hyperconnectivity and multitasking... also shows how to free ourselves from them"

Nélida and Jorge Colapinto

The brain is wider than the sky,
For, put them side by side,
The one the other will include
With ease, and you beside.
The brain is deeper than the sea
For, hold them, blue to blue,
The one the other will absorb,
As sponges, buckets do.

Emily Dickinson (1830–1886)

There is time enough for everything, in the
course of the day, if you do but one thing at once;
but there is not time enough in the year, if you
will do two things at a time... The steady and
undissipated attention to one object is a sure
mark of a superior genius; as hurry, bustle and
agitation are the never-failing symptoms of a
weak and frivolous mind.

Lord Chesterfield April (1694-1773)

It's not that I'm so smart; it's just that I stay with
problems longer.

Albert Einstein (1879-1955)

So a great intellect sinks to the level of an
ordinary one, as soon as it is interrupted and
disturbed, its attention distracted and drawn
off from the matter in hand; for its superiority
depends upon its power of concentration — of
bringing all its strength to bear upon one theme,
in the same way as a concave mirror collects into
one point all the rays of light that strike upon it.

Arthur Schopenhauer: On Noise. 1851

HOW TO
UNCHAIN
YOUR BRAIN

Unleash the full potential
of your brain
in a hyperconnected
multitasking world

A CONCISE VERSION
OF THE BESTSELLER **"BRAINCHAINS"**

Prof Dr Theo Compernolle
Compublications 2017

ISBN: 978-90-822058-5-5

ILLUSTRATIONS: Huw Aaron (contact@huwaaron.com)

EDITORS: Brittani Mann and Jim Maier

FORMATTING: Brenda Van Niekerk

DESIGN: Ivan Stojić (stojagrozny@gmail.com)

Cartoon on page 111 is an idea of Serge Diekstra

MORE INFORMATION: **www.brainchains.info**

Please send your feedback, comments, edits or questions to
comments@brainchains.info

For a custom made private label version for your employees or
customers: discount@compublications.com

Abbreviations:

ICT: Information and Communication Technology. The hardware
and software you use to find and distribute information such as
your smartphone, tablet, computer, email, browser, social media etc.

AbC: Always being connected (AbC) to the internet, constantly
checking emails, texts, news, social media, voice mails via your
phone, your tablet, your computer, etc.

Contents

About the Author

Prof Dr Theo Compernolle MD., PhD. has held the positions of Suez Chair in Leadership and Personal Development at the Solvay Business School, Adjunct Professor at INSEAD, Visiting Professor at several business schools and Professor at the Free University of Amsterdam.

He is an Adjunct Professor at the CEDEP European Centre for Executive Development in Fontainebleau (France)

As a medical doctor, neuropsychiatrist and scholar with decades of experience, he integrates science from many domains. For this book, he studied over 600 publications.

As a lecturer and trainer for audiences of all levels of education, he knows how to make this knowledge simple to understand and practical to apply. He usually gets maximum satisfaction scores. See www.compernolle.com

He consults, teaches and coaches professionals and executives in a wide range of multinational companies and business schools on four continents.

He wrote three non-fiction best-sellers in Dutch.

Introduction

This book is a concise version of my book **"BrainChains. Discover your brain and unleash its full potential in a hyperconnected world"**.

Why did I burn the midnight candle to summarize the 450 pages of "BrainChains" into 50 pages?

When "BrainChains" became a bestseller, I discovered an interesting paradox.

"BrainChains" is about how to fully develop the synergy between your brilliant brain and your amazing Information and Communication Technology (ICT), to become more intellectually productive and creative and less stressed.

However, the people who needed my book the most to become more efficient, didn't have the time to read a comprehensive book to understand how to use their brain to become more efficient.

Knowing the strengths and weaknesses of the human brain, you will get the best results from your brain-ICT synergy and become measurably more productive, more creative, in less time and with less stress.

My secret goal is that by applying the knowledge from this summary, you will become so much more efficient, that you will have time to read more books, whether to gain in depth knowledge on a subject important for your personal development or just for fun.

Good luck!

Theo Compernolle

There is nothing wrong with the technology!

The problem is the way we use these great tools!

Your future depends on the synergy between your brain and your technology

What is your MOST IMPORTANT TOOL to be successful as a professional?

Our modern Information and Communication Technology (ICT) is an incredible source of information. However, information does not equal knowledge. Knowledge, insight and creativity, require sustained and undisturbed effort, attention and concentration to find relevant information and to process it. Information is ubiquitous and is virtually free, but reflection is getting rare and precious.

In my workshops and presentations, when I ask professionals: "What is your most important tool to be successful as a professional?" 99%, all over the world, answer, "My Brain". When I then ask: "What do you know about your brain that is really practical and useful in order to get the best out of it?" The answer from 99% boils down to "Nothing" and a few urban myths.

Thus, by not knowing how your brain functions, you fail to harness the unmatched potential of the combination of your brain with your ICT to improve your productivity, creativity, well-being and prosperity.

In this condensed version of "BrainChains", I explain a few basic directions for use of your brain, such as:

- how "always being connected" ruins your intellectual productivity and why

- how multitasking of intellectual work requires between four and ten times more time for a significantly worse and less creative result

- how your archiving-brain does its job while you pause or sleep ... and much more

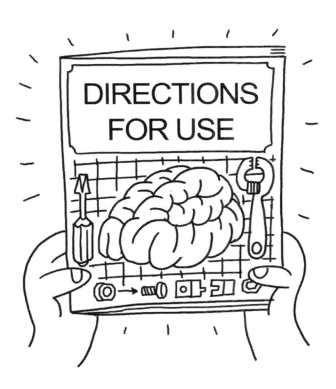

ALL EMPLOYEES ARE BRAINWORKERS, and should be the master, not the slave of their ICT

Machines replaced muscle-work. Computers took over more and more intellectual tasks. What's left for people is work needing the highest human intellectual and social skills. ALL employees are **"brainworkers"** now! I don't use the term "knowledge workers" because it usually excludes operators and administrative workers who are brainworkers too. Your most important success factor is having a good brain, knowing how to use it efficiently and effectively and developing the social-skills to connect with other brainworkers.

You can use your ICT in two ways: as a successful professional and as a consistently connected consumer.

As a successful brainworker: **You use** your ICT, paying undivided attention to find, process, produce and create relevant information. **You decide**, what you do, why, when and how long to achieve success.

By contrast, as an always connected consumer, **Your ICT uses you**, capturing your attention, aimless and effortless, with an aimless, endless stream of interesting but irrelevant information. **Your ICT decides**, what you do, why, when and how long. Companies cunningly develop addictive apps to hold your attention, for their success, not yours.

Have fun, but don't mix the two roles. It can be fatal for your intellectual productivity.

OUR FUTURE: the synergy between brilliant human brains and fantastic technology

On March 2, 2004, one of my clients, the European Space Agency, launched the satellite Rosetta. They planned to drop an explorer on the Churyumov– Gerasimenko comet, a block of ice with a diameter of 2.5 miles (4 km) speeding at (24.600 miles/h (40.000 km/h) through the Milky Way, in the neighborhood of Jupiter. Scientists compared the task to a fly trying to land on a speeding bullet.

It took the spacecraft 10 years to travel an accumulative distance of 4 billion miles (6.5 milliard kilometers) and it landed the explorer Philae within a 328 feet (100 m) area of precision.

The point I want to make, is that the network of 2000 people who assisted in the mission could never have done this without computers, AND that all the computers of the world combined could never have done this without the network of 2000 superb human thinking brains.

The essence of the ICT revolution is that, *together,* modern ICT and the unique ability of our brain to think, can produce insights, knowledge and performances that cannot be produced separately. ICT amplifies and multiplies the power of our brain.

The future lies in the synergy between the human brain and our technology. We are only at the very beginning of this synergy. Not even the sky is the limit.

THE WAY WE USE ICT in daily life UNDERMINES the potential of both our brain and our ICT

In day-to-day life, the way you use your ICT, instead of amplifying your brainpower, severely undermines it and decreases your intellectual productivity, efficiency and creativity. Lots of research supports this conclusion, but you know this already.

Could a surgeon perform high-quality surgery while being interrupted dozens of times per hour to answer a phone or to write a text or an email or to check Facebook? Of course not, and neither can a pianist, a golf player, a manager, an office worker or a mechanic.

"Always being connected", and the resulting multitasking required because of it, severely compromises your intellectual productivity, creativity and safety.

The problem is not in the extraordinary technology itself, but how you are using it without also taking into account the most fantastic tool at your disposal: your brain.

The ICT revolution unfolded so fast that, in our day-to-day life, we have yet to learn how to make the best use of the potential synergy between our ICT and our brainwork.

Moreover, capitalizing on your ignorance about your brain and ICT, companies shrewdly develop addictive apps. You let their ICT ruin your intellectual productivity.

You need basic knowledge about your brain to get the best out of it and your ICT

YOUR BRAIN is zillions of times MORE POWERFUL than any existing technology today

To make an extremely primitive model of one human brain-cortex with today's technology, you need a computer as large as the biggest Airbus hangar. It would weigh 40,000 tons and would need to consume the power of four nuclear power plants.

Do you know that there are about 160 billion brain cells that help us process data? There are so many that counting them accurately is impossible. Just compare that with the number of people on earth (7.5 billion) or stars in the Milky Way (100-400 billion). The processing and memorizing of this data does not happen in the cells, but rather in the ever-changing connections (called synapses) between cells.

Do you know that the brain-cells (neurons) which play the leading role in information processing have 1,000 to 400,000 connections with other brain cells? Even at an average of a mere 1,000, this results in 80 trillion connections. Imagine how many potential combinations are possible with 80 trillion connections. It's nearly infinite.

At these synapses "vesicles", bubbles full of chemicals, play the role of transistors in a chip. If on average 50 of them are active, we have 400 quadrillion active "transistors". You carry this "near-infinite" computing power in your "portable" brain that is half the size of a football, weighing 3 pounds (1.5 kg) and consuming 30 watts, instead of the 40,000 tons of hardware and the 4.5 Gigawatt a computer would need to mimic your brain in a very primitive way.

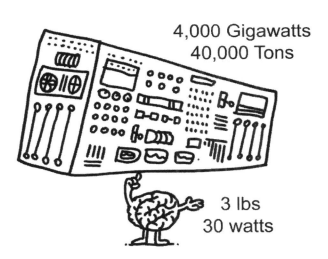

4,000 Gigawatts
40,000 Tons

3 lbs
30 watts

THREE BRAINS determine your thoughts and actions

There are three brain-networks that play a role in your thinking, decision-making and actions.

1. Your **thinking-brain** is young in evolutionary terms. Only humans can think about things that are out of the reach of our senses, that are abstract. This is the basis of language that makes it possible to pass on ever-increasing knowledge from one person to another, from one generation to the other. Only humans can contemplate the past and combine memories from the past to find a solution for today or tomorrow. We can make plans for the future. We can think in terms of "what if?", develop a hypothesis. We can postpone a decision, give it some more thought, and we can invent new things and worlds in the realm of our own imagination.

Crucial "spoiler" for the rest of this book:

**YOUR THINKING BRAIN
CAN ONLY PAY ATTENTION
TO ONE THING AT A TIME.**

2. Your **reflex-brain**, is about as old as animal existence. Even very primitive animals developed reflexes. The world of the reflex-brain is the here and now, the experience you are having in the moment using all the senses available to you. Your reflex brain has no future and no past. If something is out of the reach of your senses, it simply ceases to exist.

3. Your **archiving brain** that stores the zillions of bits of information you process every day. It continuously filters, reorganizes and stores information, when your thinking brain relaxes, especially when you sleep.

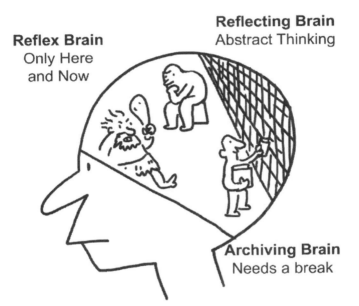

Reflecting Brain
Abstract Thinking

Reflex Brain
Only Here
and Now

Archiving Brain
Needs a break

YOUR BODY-BRAIN: connected to every single cell of your body

Before we discuss the three parts of your brain that help you to think and act, a short note about your body-brain. Your brain communicates with every single one of the 50-100 trillion cells in your body, to adapt unremittingly to internal and external changes. It does this autonomously, on auto-pilot. Every cell is like a little computer that influences and is influenced by trillions of other computers. Together they process billions of routines in tandem. They lead each other and they decide together in a complex network that works at astonishing speed. It's like an "internet of things", but much bigger, fool-proof and sophisticated beyond anything technology can realize and nobody can hack it.

The branches of your body-brain run through the whole body. They direct the working and the multiplication of all the cells; they even influence the genes in your cells. Additionally, the cells in your body give feedback to your body-brain so that it can adapt and adjust efficiently at a high speed. Your biological clock synchronizes all this activity. You can read much more about this very important clock in "BrainChains".

Your body-brain influences every single cell in your body via three systems. **Your nervous system,** which reacts super-fast, via electrical currents. **Your endocrine system,** which reacts more slowly, sending hormones as its messengers via the bloodstream. **Your immune system,** which is a sophisticated defense system that protects you against intruders such as dangerous germs and against rebels such as cancer cells.

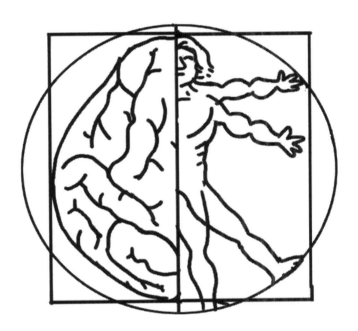

Your THINKING BRAIN is uniquely human, very sophisticated and slow

The development of the ability to interrupt our stimulus provoked reflex reactions, to pause and reflect about our goals, is a true revolution in the evolution of humankind.

The most important and uniquely human quality, of the thinking brain is that we can reflect about things that are not actually present or available to our senses. We can even fantasize and invent new ideas and things. This abstract thinking is also the foundation of language, of our ability to communicate about complex and abstract subjects like science and religions. Thanks to language, we can learn from each other and continuously expand our knowledge via conversations, writing and reading. This brain is responsible for conscious reflecting, logical, analytical and synthetic thinking, creative thinking, problem solving, thinking ahead, reflecting on the past and the future, and deep thinking.

This thinking brain is slow, it needs sustained attention and concentration. Therefore it consumes a lot of energy and becomes tired easily. For the purpose of this book, it is important to emphasize again that the thinking brain can only pay attention to one subject at a time.

The thinking brain can plan ahead, set future goals and be proactive,, something that no other animal is capable of. For these reasons, psychologists sometimes call it the "goal-oriented brain", in contrast to the "stimulus-driven" reflex brain.

One of the things that is uniquely human about the thinking brain is that it can take precedence over our reflex brain. For this reason, researchers also call it the control network, the controlling brain or the executive brain.

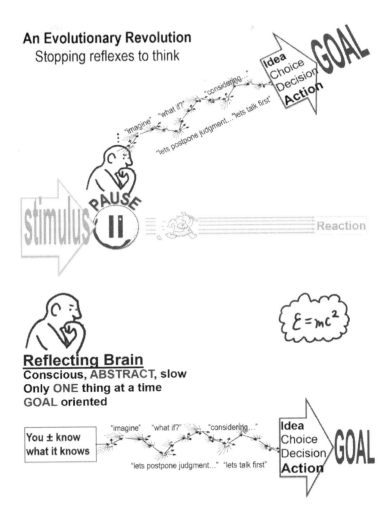

An Evolutionary Revolution
Stopping reflexes to think

GOAL

Idea
Choice
Decision
Action

"imagine" "what if?" "considering..."
"lets postpone judgment..." "lets talk first"

stimulus **PAUSE** **II**

Reaction

$\mathcal{E} = mc^2$

Reflecting Brain
Conscious, ABSTRACT, slow
Only **ONE** thing at a time
GOAL oriented

You ± know
what it knows

"imagine" "what if?" "considering..."
"lets postpone judgment..." "lets talk first"

Idea
Choice
Decision
Action

GOAL

YOUR SUCCESS depends on your ability to REFLECT

To make the best and most proactive choices and decisions in our complex, unpredictable and rapidly changing modern environment we cannot and should not give the upper hand to the primitive, unconscious, fast, but thoughtless reflex brain.

For our ancestors in the Savannah, in their daily struggle for survival, the reflex brain served them well as they did not have the time to consider many interpretations or possible actions.

To be successful in our 21st century jungle, however, we frequently need to get out of reflex mode and take the time to reflect and have real conversations. We also need to relax and disconnect periodically, to let our archiving brain deal with all the data that has been stored.

Electronic systems can only hold data and sometimes information if the data are ordered in a meaningful and accessible way. The only place where knowledge, insight and meaning reside is in people's brains. We need reflection to turn information into knowledge and wisdom, and to fulfill the tremendous synergy between our brain and our ICT.

To be successful, you need lifelong learning. Learning is the result of study, thorough reading, real conversations, undisturbed reflection and especially of trial and error. To be successful you need to take the time to debrief your errors and successes, to reflect, look backwards and forwards, and think broadly and deeply.

INFORMATION
is abundant and cheap

REFLECTION
is rare and precious

MULTITASKING: a key-concept to understand the most important BrainChain

There are two kinds of multitasking. The first is "simultaneous multitasking", defined as trying to do two things at the same time, like doing emails while participating in a conference call. The second is "serial multitasking", defined as doing parts of many different tasks one after the other; for example, taking a break from writing an important memo to answer a few emails, respond to your voicemail etc. and then returning to your memo.

The distinction between these two forms of multitasking is useful, but for your thinking brain, there is no distinction because in both cases it is constantly switching between tasks. Later I will discuss a special kind of simultaneous multitasking where your reflex-brain takes care of the routine while your thinking brain is on standby for non-routine events or free to reflect on other subjects.

Multitasking is a concept that comes from the computer world. It means that a serial-processor, the heart of most computers, can only do one task at any one time, but switches so fast between several tasks that it seems to be doing all these tasks simultaneously. To do that it briefly stores the information into a temporary memory, which is like a whiteboard. It has a limited capacity. Once it's full, you have to erase the old stuff to make room for new ideas. As we will see, this metaphor is useful to understand what's happening in our brain when we try to multitask.

PARALLEL MULTITASKING

Task 1

Task 2

SERIAL MULTITASKING

Task 1   Task 2   Task 3   Task 2   Task 3   Task 1

Do you think MULTITASKING IS EFFICIENT AND SAFE?

Back to our question: Do you think the surgeon operating on you, or the car mechanic fixing your brakes can do a thorough and safe job when there are other tasks interrupting them every three minutes? Do you think *you* can do your job well while switching between tasks all the time?

Imagine you are refurbishing part of your house and while you are painting a wall you think "I might need bigger screws later". Immediately you stop painting, close the paint-can, clean your brush, drive to the hardware store, buy the screws, drive home, open the can and continue with your paint job.

5 minutes later you think "I'm almost out of beer". You stop painting, close the paint-can, clean your brush, drive to the supermarket, buy beer... 5 minutes later "I might need a smaller brush to finish". You stop painting, close the paint-can... And so, you continue like this, interrupting the big painting job every few minutes to buy sanding paper, potatoes, milk, etc.

Is this efficient? productive? clever? Certainly not, and still that's exactly how a majority of brainworkers do their work! So you know that multitasking is not a productive, efficient, creative nor safe way to do your work. But, you probably didn't know that your thinking brain simply cannot multitask and that if you attempt it nevertheless, you lose a lot of time, accuracy, memory, creativity, productivity, and efficiency; as well, you experience more stress.

Did you know that

Thirty minutes of uninterrupted work is

- three times more efficient than three times ten minutes;
- four times more efficient if the tasks are complex;
- ten times more efficient than ten stints of three minutes.

Did you know that

- most professionals have more than 65 open tasks?
- spend 3 to 11 minutes on a task before being interrupted?
- after a distraction, it takes them 25 minutes to return to the original task?
- in 40% of situations they don't even return to the original task?

Efficient??? Productive??? Clever???

This is even no longer multitasking but hypertasking.

NOT CONVINCED multitasking is extremely inefficient? Do an EXPERIMENT.

Take a piece of paper, a pen and a watch or stopwatch. The test consists of two very simple tasks. In the first round you single-task: you do the first task and when finished, do the second one. In the second round, you multitask: you switch back and forth between the two tasks.

For each round, you measure how long it takes.

First round: Single-tasking.

Write "SINGLETASKING" in capital letters and then immediately write each letter's serial number underneath and stop the stopwatch. The result looks like:

S	I	N	G	L	E	T	A	S	K	I	N	G
1	2	3	4	5	6	7	8	9	10	11	12	13

Second round: Multitasking.

Write "MULTITASKING" one letter at a time and then immediately write its corresponding number underneath. You will write M then 1, U then 2, L then 3, T 4, I 5 etc...

M	U	L	T	I	T	etc...
1	2	3	4	5	6	

On average the multitasking takes double the time, a third of people make a mistake while multitasking and everybody feels more stressed while doing it.

Imagine what you lose in the black hole of multitasking when you are switching constantly, not between two super-simple tasks, but between nonroutine, complex work and a dozen tasks and chores. It's pathetic what you lose in efficiency, productivity and creativity.

FROM HOMO SAPIENS TO HOMO ZAPPIENS
TO HOMO INTERRUPTUS

You cannot train or change your **reflecting** brain to multitask

600 million years
from first brain to singletasking human brain

30 years of cognitive
multitasking=1/20 millionth
of history of brain

TASK-SWITCHING aka serial multitasking

Let me explain why multitasking is so inefficient. Imagine you are concentrating on a difficult and complex task. This means your working-memory handles the task. Then you see the pop-up screen announcing an email. You decide it's a simple question that you can answer quickly and decide to work on it.

For your brain, it's not simple at all. Your brain must now move all the complex, rich information from your working memory to your temporary memory, clean your working memory (otherwise the two tasks will interfere), and move the information you need for the e-mail from your long-term memory to your working memory. Then you need to build up your concentration to answer the mail. When you go back to the original task, your brain goes through the same process.

The average office worker, once distracted by email, rarely looks at only one email. It takes on average 11 emails before he or she gets back to the original task. Hence for every email you go through the same process. You can imagine that this takes a lot of time and energy. Moreover, your temporary memory is limited, and it's "first in, first out" so that information from your difficult complex task is pushed out, especially if you were so busy that you archiving brain did not have a chance to properly store it. You can imagine that a lot of information falls between the cracks and that it causes more stress.

To make it even worse, the more different the contexts you are switching between the bigger the loss.

SERIAL MULTITASKING: BIG LOSS OF PERFORMANCE

Switch

Task 1 ——————▶

Task 2 ▶

- ✓ Stop task 1
- ✓ Move data task 1 from Work M to Temp M
- ✓ Clean Working Memory
- ✓ Load data 2 from Long M or Temp M into Work M
- ✓ Build-up concentration

Result = switching-cost: huge loss of time, memory, quality and energy

Every interruption is a switch!

People in open offices are interrupted every minute!
PRODUCTIVITY DISAPPEARS
IN THE BLACK HOLE OF SWITCHING!

Doing TWO THINGS AT THE SAME time aka simultaneous multitasking

By doing simultaneous multitasking, like writing emails while participating in a conference call, you are constantly switching back and forth between the two tasks from different contexts. By switching you lose information and energy, create more stress and make many more stupid mistakes.

But, it's even worse than that. Most people think they can pay partial attention to one task while attending to another. Since your thinking brain can only pay attention to one task at a time, **your attention is fractured**, not partial! While you are writing an email, **you do NOT hear what's being said** in the conference call. It is easy to identify those whose attention is fractured. They are the people who ask questions already asked or give answers already given. Believing you can give full attention to both the conference AND the email is an illusion and if, after reading this, you still believe you are an exception, it becomes a delusion.

But it's even worse. Our brain does not like these sudden gaps in the flow of information. It will try to fill in the gaps by guessing. As a result, **you hear things that nobody said.** When you know the subject of the conference call and the people discussing it very well, your brain might sometimes guess right and this will reinforce your illusion that you can have partial attention. More often than you think, however, your brain will guess wrong. You will hear conclusions, statements and agreements that nobody made.

For example: writing emails while in a conference call

Problem #1: you are continuously SWITCHING

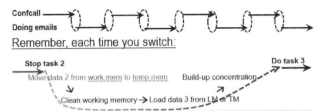

Confcall

Doing emails

Remember, each time you switch:

Stop task 2

Do task 3

Move data 2 from work mem to temp mem   Build-up concentration

Clean working memory → Load data 3 from LM or TM

RESULT: LOSS OF ENERGY, MEMORY, REFLECTION, UNDERSTANDING ETC...

Problem #2: Partial attention = ILLUSION & DELUSION

Reflecting Brain → **ONE** "channel" at a time

The reality = **FRACTURED** attention

YOU DO NOT HEAR WHAT IS BEING SAID !

Problem #3: your brain fills the gaps guessing !

GUESS → GUESS → GUESS → GUESS →

GUESS → GUESS → GUESS → GUESS →

YOU HEAR THINGS THAT WERE NOT SAID !

CONCLUSION for the modern Homo Interruptus: Radically, Ruthlessly ERADICATE SWITCHES

It's extraordinary what your thinking brain can do, but there is one thing it can't do: multitask. It can only pay attention to one thing at a time. Doing two cognitive tasks at the same time is impossible. If you try it regardless, you continuously switch between tasks. This juggling of information costs you dearly in time, energy, accuracy, memory, creativity, productivity and stress.

Further on I will explain that being able to always connect is fantastic for your brainwork, but that always being connected is a disaster for the quantity and quality of your intellectual work. The major reason is that always being connected is THE major cause of continuous multitasking.

Moreover, your brain's attention goes directly to what's important for your primitive reflex brain but not always to what's important for your rational thinking brain. If you don't respect the needs of your thinking brain, your reflex brain will too often decide for you.

The remedy is simple, but often difficult to execute. *Radically, ruthlessly eradicate switches.* This requires creativity and initially a bit of discipline and willpower. Once you systematically do this, the rewards are huge. Therefore, if you want to get the best results from your thinking brain: eliminate the interruptions, primarily by regularly disconnecting from your ICT, and avoid working in open plan offices where distraction is frequent.

THE FIRST COMMANDMENT

Ruthlessly, Radically
ERADICATE SWITCHES

Your archiving brain and your thinking brain NEED IDLING

Your archiving-brain uses the same working memory, or "brain-microprocessor", as your thinking brain. Your archiving brain is continuously active, using the tiniest little bit of processor space possible to do its work. It can only archive when your thinking brain slows down, or takes a break, and most importantly when you sleep.

Therefore, filling in your so-called "lost moments" with "busyness" on your smartphone, tablet or computer is very counterproductive and detrimental to the development of knowledge and understanding. It is a killer for your creativity. When I ask participants "When and where do you have your most creative ideas or sudden insights", they often answer: while jogging, in the shower, in bed, never "at work"!? What do all these situations have in common:

1. These individuals took time for study and reflection and thereby were able to draw on the knowledge stored in their long-term memory. It's exactly this reflection time that is lost when people are always connected.

2. They were relaxed: their archiving brain had ample "processor time" to find and recombine information. Always being connected jeopardizes this too.

3. They were disconnected, not consciously thinking hard about the issue or problem at hand.

Nietzsche once said: "All great ideas come from walking." If Steve Jobs had been as overly consumed with his iPhone like you, he never would have had invented the iPhone.

Archiving Brain

SLEEP: one of the MOST IMPORTANT sources of intellectual productivity, creativity and health

You need sufficient sleep:

- to recuperate physically
- to restore the energy your thinking brain needs -to let your archiving brain reorder and store all the information you took in during the day
- to develop new brain cells (especially for your longterm memory) and to form new connections between them
- to break down and eliminate the waste products your brain produced during the day
- to process, maintain or restore your emotional stability
- to activate processes for which there is not enough surplus energy during the day, such as growing, repairing, rejuvenating, restoring your immune system and much more.

Most people need between 7 and 8 hours of sleep to function at their best. Your biological clock needs sufficient sleep to regulate the function of a dozen hormones that regulate your weight, blood sugar, growth, heart, sex and much more.

If you don't sleep enough your body may still be able to cope because it recuperates primarily in the first half of the night, but your archiving brain will suffer the most because it works more in the second half of your sleep, and that's the part you cut off when you don't sleep enough. Further on I describe two ways to find out how much sleep you **really** need.

For additional tips on how to develop healthy sleeping habits, see 377 in my book "BrainChains".

Your primitive REFLEX-BRAIN: its speed may jeopardize your rational thinking

Your fully reactive "stimulus-driven" system is also a "snapshot brain" because its conclusions are based on what you experience with your senses here and now. "Sensory Now" is all that exists for it.

Your primitive reflex brain reacts much faster than your thinking brain because it can process inputs from all of your senses simultaneously. It works with many genetic shortcuts and acquired habits to do so. This was a big advantage for your ancestors in their life or death struggle throughout the evolution of mankind. Yet it's a liability in the jungle of the 21st century. If you don't support your thinking brain to check your reflex-brain's rapid conclusions, your reflex brain makes a lot of irrational mistakes.

Your reflex brain allows you to develop ever more complex automated behavior like playing a piano, driving a car, etc. A problem for brainworkers, is that the attention of your reflex-brain is unconsciously captured by novel or sudden sensory changes, in the work setting mostly sights and sounds. This interferes with the conscious attention that your thinking brain needs, and with the time your archiving brain needs to store the information in your memory. What's more, each time a stimulus captures the attention of your reflex brain you get a little shot of dopamine in your brain. This works like a drug. Dopamine belongs to the family of amphetamine. It urges you to seek out these stimuli and maybe even become addicted to them

SPEED:
The Worst Enemy
of Reflection.

The first secret of the speed of your reflex brain: INNATE SHORTCUTS

Your reflex-brain is fast not only because Sensory Now is all it knows, but also because it uses innate shortcuts called cognitive biases and heuristics. It is worthwhile to learn about them because they tend to be the reason why you frequently make stupid decision. Also because marketers, app-builders and especially social media outlets exploit them to glue you to your screen, make you spend more money and give away as much private information as possible.

Scientists have described more than a 100 of them. Just a few examples

When you have to choose between three similar products with three different prices, your reflex brain will automatically choose the middle price one and your thinking brain will usually go along with this. You can imagine how easy it is for sales people to exploit this bias. Did you know that managers make very different decisions when they discuss a million dollar purchase first and then one that costs tens of thousands, as opposed to doing it the other way around?

The Instant Gratification bias makes you choose the immediate reward ignoring the long-term cost. The Sunk Cost fallacy will make you spend more money after you invested in something even if it seems like a wrong decision. Scarcity bias will increase your desire to buy something if the seller mentions, "Only three left." The Bias bias makes you think you are less influenced by biases than other people are.

Reflex Brain

Unconscious, here and now, **VERY FAST**
All senses at the same time
Stimulus driven

The second secret of the speed of your reflex brain: LEARNED SHORTCUTS, habits

When you learn to drive a car all the information about what you have to do is processed by your thinking brain, which can only handle one task at a time. Consequently, when you are thinking about braking, you forget the clutch; when you think about the clutch, you forget to look in your mirror etc. At first you feel hopeless and overwhelmed that there are too many things to think about at the same time. You are left with a feeling of "I will never learn this". Indeed, if you only had your thinking brain, you would never manage.

When you keep practicing, however, after many frustrating hours, many mistakes and receiving immediate feedback, such as the car stalling, your reflex brain gradually develops "soft-wired shortcuts", a new habit.

The conscious knowledge gradually transfers to your reflex brain where it becomes an unconscious routine and driving becomes a habit. Your reflex brain can then process many inputs very quickly at the same time while your thinking brain is on standby for the non-routine, the unexpected. It can also think about other things.

The same transfer to our reflex-brain happened with hundreds of routines we perform daily, without thinking.

This works so well, that many people even think that they can safely talk on the phone while driving, but as I will explain further on that's an extremely dangerous mistake.

Reflective-Reflex collaboration after long practice

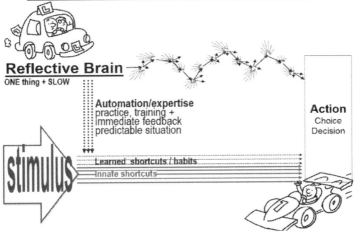

Reflective Brain
ONE thing + SLOW

Automation/expertise
practice, training +
immediate feedback
predictable situation

stimulus

Learned shortcuts / habits
Innate shortcuts

Action
Choice
Decision

EMOTIONS are powerful, fast reflexes LABELLED AFTER THE FACT by your thinking brain

In general, intense emotions tend to shortcut the thinking brain, diverting us from our goal to the immediately present stimuli, leading among other things to automatic reactions. This is an excellent mechanism when lightning fast action is required, but can be a problem when a little reflection would lead to much better choices, decisions and actions.

Often a situation triggers an emotional reflex in your brain and then in the rest of your body (e.g. heart beating, flushing, trembling, tensing muscles). Only after some delay, your thinking brain considers the situation, and labels these reactions, after the fact, as an emotion e.g. anger. However, your fast reflex brain might already have provoked a behavioral reaction before your slower thinking brain becomes aware of these sensations.

Hence, your reflex brain often affects your behavior more than it should.

Moreover, your thinking brain needs energy and easily tires. Hence, its modulating effect on emotions diminishes throughout the day. Thus, the cruder basic reactions like aggression and anxiety arising from the untiring reflex brain become more outspoken in the evening, especially if we don't take sufficient breaks, are tired from working in an open office or don't sleep enough.

Luckily, through unrelenting education and life experiences you develop soft-wired shortcuts, habits, which help to modulate, control or even contain your reflex emotional reactions and behavior.

EMOTIONS are also TRIGGERED by your thinking brain

Sometimes your thinking brain itself is the source of the emotion. In many situations, the way you assess the situation triggers your behavioral, emotional and physical reactions.

If you interpret a comment from your boss as an aggressive, unjustified criticism from a pretentious nobody, there is a good chance that you will feel angry and your heart might start beating faster while your blood pressure goes up and you might behave in a defensive or hostile manner towards him. To feel angry, you don't even need the presence of your boss. You can become angry later when you are just thinking about what happened or while you are explaining it to your spouse. It is also possible that you will feel angry again when you start thinking about the incident months later.

If you had interpreted his comment more sympathetically, for example as a normal reaction of a very insecure person, you would have felt very different. The stress would have been lower or non-existent and your behavior would have been different, for example perhaps even supportive.

A good actor who really gets into the character can feel the emotions that go with the role, just by imagining himself in that situation.

This insight that thoughts cause feelings, physiological reactions and behavior is the basis of an impressive amount of research in the field known as cognitive psychology.

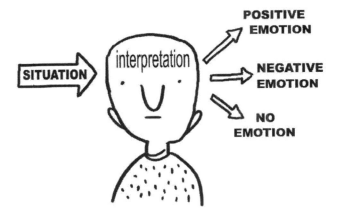

When your TWO BRAINS COMPETE, your thinking brain is the underdog

Most often, the two brains collaborate well and to our advantage. The reflex brain is at its best in familiar routine situations. It will come up with a very fast answer and then leave it to the thinking brain to accept it or not. The way the reflex brain takes care of routines by turning them into habits frees up our thinking brain for reflection. As I will explain further on, working together they can multitask.

Sometimes the two brains compete. For example, a professional football player does not think about how to pass the ball. After lots of training, this became a highly skilled unconscious routine. However, when he fails a few times and starts worrying, the negative thoughts of the thinking brain get in the way of the reflex brain and what before came naturally now goes wrong.

On the other hand, and more importantly for your intellectual productivity, the fast reflex brain often gets ahead of the thinking brain when you do intellectual work.

This is very often the case when you are continuously connected or multitasking or your thinking brain is tired. Your thinking brain consumes quite a lot of energy. It easily becomes exhausted, while your reflex brain never tires. Because of this handicap, your reflex brain is quick to take the lead when you are tired. It's the story of the tortoise and the hare except that this hare never sleeps and this tortoise does.

An Evolutionary Revolution
Blocked by Always Being Connected

Take good care of your thinking brain, otherwise your primitive REFLEX BRAIN WILL DECEIVE YOU

If you don't deliberately take time to reflect, your reflex brain will guess and often guess wrong especially when you are in a hurry or stressed. It will lead you to rapid but primitive if not stupid conclusions and decisions. Do you remember the biases and heuristics I described before? That's how. Other examples are:

Due to the **Availability-bias**, makes you overestimate the likelihood of rare events: you will be more afraid of dying in a terrorist attack (a chance of 1/2,000,000,000) than driving a car (a chance of 1/15,000). The **Bandwagon effect** makes you follow group-think even if it's stupid and the **Loss Aversion bias** makes you hold onto a bad investment or decision for no good reason, etc...

Whenever you fail to take care of the needs of your thinking brain or keep it shackled by the BrainChains I will describe later, the reflex brain takes the lead. This often makes deciding much faster and simpler in rather straightforward, simple, predictable situations that you know from experience.

However, it will lead to very bad decisions when the situation is new or very complex, unpredictable or when numbers and statistics are important for the decision. This is a problem in a fast-paced working environment, where people are always connected, where there is no time for reflection and every break is used to gobble up new information.

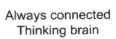

Always connected
Thinking brain

Primitive
Reflex Brain

The ONLY POSSIBLE MULTITASKING: a collaboration between your thinking brain and your reflex brain

If you inferred from the previous chapters that your thinking brain can multitask in collaboration with your reflex brain, you are perfectly right. While your reflex brain takes care of the routines, your thinking brain can pay attention to other things.

When you first learn to play the piano, it's hard thinking about how to do different things with both hands. But if, after hundreds of hours of training, this part of the job is taken over by the reflex brain, and you don't have to think about your fingers hitting the right notes anymore, your thinking brain is now free to fully concentrate on the interpretation. Then after another few hundred hours of playing, you don't have to think about how you want the piece to sound. Now it really comes from the gut (= reflex-brain). You may become so good that, even after an emotionally disturbing event, the resulting negative emotions don't disrupt your performance too much.

Your thinking brain should be on stand-by to keep improving the routine or for non-routine events, e.g. while driving or cooking. When it's not on standby because it's paying attention to your phone, you will cause an accident or burn your fingers. Your thinking brain can even concentrate on something totally different, like looking at television while knitting. However, when you drop a stitch and need to focus on that, you will miss the heroine kissing the hero, because your thinking brain can only focus on one thing at a time.

Reflective-Reflex collaboration after long practice

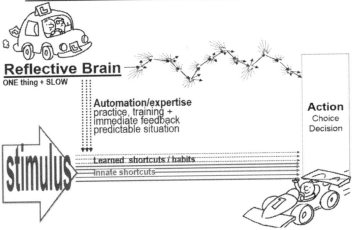

Reflective Brain →
ONE thing + SLOW

Automation/expertise
practice, training +
immediate feedback
predictable situation

Action
Choice
Decision

stimulus

Learned shortcuts / habits
Innate shortcuts

Multitasking is only possible in a collaboration between our reflecting brain and our reflex brain

While our **Reflex brain** unconsciously handles the routines

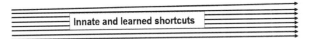

Innate and learned shortcuts

Our **Reflecting brain** can think about the non-routine

Examples: Cooking, playing a musical instrument, driving a car, playing golf or football, doing surgery, writing etc…

Five BrainChains

BRAINCHAIN #1:
Always Being Connected

The root cause of your lack of efficiency

The *opportunity* to always be connected is marvelous for our brainwork but, actually being constantly connected is a total disaster.

Modern technology allows us to always be connected, anytime and anywhere, the implication being that we choose when and where we want to connect. When these great technologies are well-used, they can indeed help us to work more effectively and efficiently and to keep in touch with more people. The reality, however, is that most professionals have switched from 'anytime, anywhere' to 'all the time, everywhere'. The freedom to choose has disappeared. People feel they *must* be connected all the time, everywhere. Hyper-connectivity has become a bad habit and in some cases even a real addiction.

The greatest peril for professionals is that hyperconnectivity ruins reflection, thorough reading, real conversations and discussions; it significantly decreases your intellectual performance. As a professional, your success does not depend on your ability to consume information but on the way that you intelligently process, produce and create information.

When you are continuously reacting to texts, emails, voicemails and social media, and constantly receiving information from the outside world there is no time or space left for your brain to process the information, to store it in your memory, to play around with your own ideas, to be creative, or to reflect.

For your intellectual productivity and creativity

Always able to connect is fantastic !

What a freedom!
- ✓ You are in control of your ICT.
- ✓ You choose.
- ✓ You can connect with anyone, any time, anywhere.
- ✓ You batch-task.

Always connected is a disaster !!

No freedom,
- ✓ **Your ICT controls you**
- ✓ **Your ICT chooses**
- ✓ You think **you must connect** with everybody, all the time and everywhere
- ✓ **You multitask continuously**

Bad habit? Neurotic? Really addicted?

13 Problems caused by ALWAYS BEING CONNECTED (AbC)

1. *AbC is a weapon of mass distraction.* To be intellectually productive you need to give a topic your undivided attention, protecting your reflecting-brain from distractions. (More further on))

2. *AbC puts your brain into a continuous impulsive reactive mode.* Your reflex brain gets the upper hand and your decisions become "ad hoc" snapshots that are less discriminating and less accurate than decisions reached when you're using your thinking brain.

3. *AbC crowds out the sometimes duller but usually much more important brainwork of reflection,* including thinking ahead, thinking broadly, going deep into a subject and remembering it.

4. *AbC turns employees into "adhocrats" (adhocrats?) and organizations into "adhocracies"* (instead of bureaucrats and bureaucracies). Interruptiondriven, immediate, and thoughtless or rather reflection-less ad-hoc reactions crowd out planned work and reflection.

5. *AbC makes you succumb to the cognitive biases* and heuristics of your primitive reflex-brain.

6. *AbC forces multitasking* This decreases productivity, memory and creativity while increasing stress.

7. *AbC causes accidents at home, at work and on the streets.* Because you can only pay attention to one thing at a time, you are blind to the world around you when you are busy with your ICT.

We become
ADHOCRATS
in
ADHOCRAZY
ADHOCRACIES

(Replacing
Bureaucrats in
Bureaucracies)

8. *AbC causes information overload.* You no longer take the time to process all the input and to develop your own ideas. This results in an overload of information that your brain can no longer process and store in the time available. Thus it becomes impossible to make thoughtful choices and decisions, which further increases the subjective feeling of overload. This creates a continuous background of brain-stress and can be very de-motivating.

9. *AbC consumes a lot of energy that is no longer available for reflection.* A never-ending stream of small decisions consumes as much mental energy as one big important decision. You leave things to your reflex brain, postponing important decisions or making the easiest, most primitive, irrational, impulsive, bad choices.

As a result, the worst decisions, choices, mistakes and misbehaviors happen in the evening, especially if you don't take regular breaks or if you work in open offices.

10. *AbC eliminates the vital down time your archiving brain needs to store and order information.* When your thinking brain continuously works at full capacity, this does not leave enough brainpower for your archiving brain to correctly store all the information or to come up with creative ideas.

Therefore, being busy with your smartphone all the time, filling all the little gaps of "lost" time, or 'slack', with little tasks, is not smart at all; it's ignorant.

INCESSANT INPUT
of email, text and phone
makes your brain
REACTIVE

11. *AbC ruins real conversations, relations, discussions and meetings.* On the one hand, your fantastic technology allows you to connect with people you love or need, anywhere and anytime you choose. On the other hand, always being connected often gets in the way of real conversations and relations. Some people believe that they can follow a conversation while working on emails. I explained above that this is a delusion!

12. *AbC ruins off-site meetings.* During off-site meetings it is difficult for managers to disconnect from the daily, nitty-gritty, operational stuff, when they don't radically disconnect from the "site in their pocket". This results in a fragmented "grasshopper" view rather than the comprehensive helicopter view they need. Since they fill the breaks by guzzling petty data, the important information is not properly stored, creativity is down and they neglect their team-relationship. Last but not least:

13. *AbC-people are no longer in control of their life.* They disappear into their virtual world at the sound of a buzz or a ringtone. They no longer voluntarily choose to enter their virtual world, their virtual world chooses for them. They end up never being 100% present. Their thinking-brain is never fully engaged. Their productivity is low. Their relations are shallow.

Consequence for Executives
Instead of a <u>strategic helicopter view</u>

an inefficient, stressed, always connected
<u>operational grasshopper view</u>

10 Reasons why it is so DIFFICULT TO DISCONNECT

Forewarned is forearmed

1. It's fun to be connected.

Every time you react to a message, you get a little shot of the fun-hormone Dopamine in your brain. This is the reason way many people go on the internet when they are feeling a little down. When you are fully focused on one task you don't get this dopamine. Focus costs energy. But, when you finish a task it gives you a longer lasting feeling of satisfaction. The problem is that the immediate fun tends to win out over the long term satisfaction.

2. We have an innate tendency for instant gratification.

AbC can give you continuous instant gratification of your needs for novelty, for action, for pleasure, for being needed, for feeling important etc... Being able to postpone gratification, however, is very important for your success in life. In his world-famous research, Walter Michel demonstrated convincingly that children who could postpone gratification at the age of 4-6, became adults who had higher scores at school, were less likely to be obese or addicted to drugs and less likely to be divorced.

3. We have an innate tendency for developing habits.

The advantage of easily developing habits is that they make our life much simpler, so that in many situations we can act more economically, without thinking. The way we mishandle our continuous ICTconnection can also be attributed to the fact that is has become a habit. As a result, we do it without thinking and it is difficult to change the way we do it.

4. We have an innate tendency to develop conditioned reflexes.

Due to a conditioned response, Pavlov's dogs started drooling when the lab assistant who fed them appeared, even when he was not carrying any food. Pavlov later demonstrated that anything which had been presented together with the food elicited drooling even without food present. The same thing happens with the sound of your phone or the slightest feeling of being bored. These triggers make you stop whatever you are doing and reach for your phone. Important work, conversations, family activities or real life won't stop the Pavlovian reflex of connecting.

5. We have an innate tendency for a fast reaction rather than for a slow reflection.

When our prehistoric ancestors were confronted with a saber-toothed tiger, a tendency to reflect would have been self-destructive. Today, it's often the other way around: not reflecting is often selfdestructive.

6. We have an innate tendency to look for danger.

Signals of potential danger are much more powerful attention-grabbers than signals that everything is OK and humming along peacefully. Therefore, every time we receive an e-mail or message that contains bad news, or something frightening, disturbing or warning us of imminent danger, it strengthens our desire to keep checking our e-mails. The more anxious a person you are, the more often you will check.

The Offspring of Pavlov's Dogs

Before conditioning:

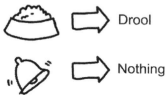

During conditioning:

After conditioning:

7. We have an innate tendency to be curious.

Curiosity as an exploratory reaction to novel objects is old in evolutionary terms, as it belongs to the reflex brain, and it does not require great effort. It is important for survival. Moreover, finding something new stimulates a brain chemical that causes excitement.

8. We have an innate tendency for addiction.

When your habit becomes an addiction, you no longer control your life, your habit controls you. You need to do it, even if it has a negative impact on more important aspects of your life. Doing it makes you feel better. Your brain produces a stimulating chemical and stopping the behavior makes you feel bad.

9. We have an innate need to belong.

It is a perfectly normal desire to want to belong, to want to be accepted by other people that are important to you. Nobody likes to be rejected. Insecure people, however, over-react with intense anxiety at the slightest snub. As a result, they suffer from what I call "Fear Of Being Excluded" or FOBE, especially on social media where being unfriended is only a mouse click away.

Instead of disconnecting from social media, they get even more compulsively involved, in vain, to find acceptance while increasing the risk of being rejected, hence creating a painful vicious cycle. This anxiety too is exploited by marketers and app builders.

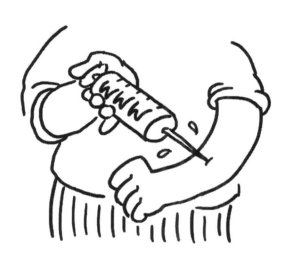

10. We tend to stay connected with what others do.

The normal need to belong can also become an exaggerated Fear Of Missing Out or FOMO: a pervasive apprehension that others might be having rewarding experiences from which you are absent. In the endless stream of irrelevant information, there will always be things you miss. For an insecure person, this reinforces the fear. It becomes a constant urge to always be connected, to always know what others are doing. Marketers and app-builders slyly exploit this fear to glue you to their products, so you can stay 'in the know'.

Conclusion: Forewarned is forearmed.

These neuropsychological mechanisms do not determine your responses, but they have a tendency to shape them.

Moreover, app-developers and marketers stealthily and slyly seduce, hook, manipulate and steal from us.

They often know these ten reasons that make it so difficult to connect, as well as scientists. They use these ten reasons in conjunction with the results of the very best neuropsychological research to seduce you, to hook you, to addict you to their products. Knowing this may help you to cut their puppet strings and disconnect regularly.

Anyway, if you are used to always being connected, it will be difficult to stop it, especially at the beginning. This is no excuse for not trying, because so many others succeeded.

**Beware of the brain-bait and brain-traps
of app developers and marketers**

BRAINCHAIN #2: Multitasking

11 reasons why it WRECKS YOUR PRODUCTIVITY

Let me shout again, loud and clear: **your thinking brain cannot multitask!** Period. When you try to multitask it has a tremendously negative impact on your intellectual productivity.

- Every task takes longer due to the interruptions.

- Every task takes longer because at each switch the slate of your working memory must be cleaned and prepared for the next task, parking the information of the first task in your temporary memory and inhibiting the first task from interfering with the second.

- It significantly decreases the quality of your work.

- It makes you drop information from your memory, and lots of information is lost because of the continuous juggling between working memory, temporary memory and long-term memory.

- It causes you to lose concentration. If you try to stay concentrated, it requires exponentially more energy.

- It causes significantly more stupid mistakes that often require more time to correct than if it had just been done right the first time.

- It kills your creativity.

- It causes unsafe behavior on the factory floor, on the streets, as well as at home.

- It makes the vitally important tasks of thorough reading and real conversations impossible.

- In the presence of others, it results in bad listening and communication skills and is often just plain rude.

- It causes more stress etc ...

BRAINCHAIN #3: Negative Stress

FRIEND AND FOE of your intellectual productivity

The more resilient you are, the better and healthier you can react to high demands.

You cannot always remove the source of stress, for example it may be inherent to your job, but you can always work to improve your resilience to it. Moreover, stress is a personal, subjective phenomenon. What causes stress for some, is seen as a challenge or a stimulant for others. If you have a negative view of stress you will experience negative stress quicker and more often. Therefore, don't forget the positive and stimulating side of stress. You need a healthy level of stress to perform at your best. It can stimulate improved performance, increased cooperation, creativity, and push you beyond your limits and help you find new solutions to old problems.

Stress can be your best friend in that under the right amount of pressure, at the right moment, it can help you to work faster and better. A lack of stress leads to boredom and the feeling that you are not making enough use of your capabilities. Therefore, a stress-free life is not what you want. Working towards a healthy balance between stress and resilience is a vital task.

It's not lots of stress, but stress without sufficient time of recuperation that makes us ill. Healthy stress is interval stress. Before you run into any risk, there are always signals, psychological and physical signals, warning you to do something about your StressBalance (see further on and in my book "Stress: Friend and Foe).

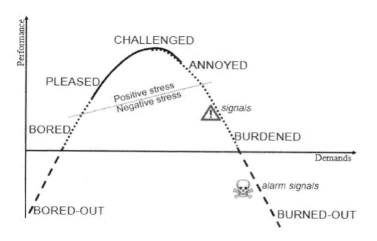

BRAINCHAIN #4:
Lack of pauses and sleep

Always wired, always tired

A lack of sleep is bad for your body and mind. It ruins your intellectual productivity, creativity and health, makes you feel less happy and appear less sexy.

"Insufficient sleep is a public health epidemic" was stated the conclusion the Centers for Disease Control and Prevention in a nationwide survey in the USA.

Because lack of sleep messes up the biological clock that coordinates all processes of our body, it increases the risk of many disorders like heart disease, infectious disorders, diabetes, obesity and especially mood disorders. Beyond the negative effects on health, it is also very bad for intellectual productivity and because of both, for national health, our companies and the economy.

Too many people see sleep as a waste of time. They stay connected too late, often because they fear they will miss something in the infinite stream of information. Many people react with a "Yes, but I work better in the evening". Indeed, from research we know that there are "Owls" and "Larks". Typical creative types are often evening people, Owls, who stay up late and wake up late. Successful professionals are often Larks who wake up early and go to bed early. In general, Larks function better and are more productive than Owls. 60% of the population fall in-between these two 'types'.

However, in most situations where I am dealing with professionals who say "I am a typical Owl" they turn out to be "Fake-Owls" who go to bed late, get up early and live with a chronic sleep debt.

Lack of sleep affects your body and mind

BODY

- Sugar tolerance ↓ thyroid hormone ↓
- Cortisol ↑ Immune system ↑↓
- Aging ↑ Weight ↑ (6h 2 × more obese >< 8h)
- Diabetes ↑ Live shorter !

BRAIN!!

- Patience ↓↓
- Feeling for nuance ↓ Insight ↓ Judgement ↓
- Concentration ↓↓ Memory ↓↓
- Creativity ↓
- Multitasking ↓
- Decision capability ↓
- Depression ↑ moodiness ↑
- Happiness ↓ Enthusiasm ↓
- Sexual desire ↓↓

SOCIAL

- Family relations ↓ Sexual relationship ↓↓
- Attractiveness ↓ Looking older ↑ etc.

BRAINCHAIN # 5: Open Plan Offices
A DISASTER for brainwork

The most important causes of distraction are related to the way you use your ICT. But there is one that is outside of your control: the open plan office. In open offices, workers are interrupted on average every three minutes. Therefore, working in an open office is a disaster for the thinking-brain of the poor modern Homo Interruptus. The cages in modern zoos are better for animals, than modern offices are for people, because modern zoo-directors know more about the innate needs of their animals than executives about the brains and the innate needs of people.

The solution is not a return to the individual rabbit cages of the past, but to have flexible offices. These are offices where the worker always finds the right kind of space for each task.

Most flexible offices have their priorities wrong. For brainwork that is not routine, the first priorities should be attention, concentration and focus. Communication comes second, not the other way around. The first priority should be to eliminate as many interruptions as possible, giving special attention to eliminating noise.

This book focuses on all the things you can do within your own area of control. Your open office is not. Therefore, I will not elaborate on this issue. If you are looking for scientific information to stimulate a discussion about the kind of offices brainworkers need to be optimally productive, you can download a free and copyright free booklet "The Open Office Is Naked" at the website www.brainchains.info tab: Free Book.

LOW PRIVACY = LOW PRODUCTIVITY !

Lack of Architectural
PRIVACY

Interruptions
Lack of Perceived Privacy:
Noise!! #1= Phone

Cognitive/emotional
Exhaustion

The cages in modern zoo's are better for animals, than modern offices for people,

the open
office

is naked

because modern ZOO-directors know more about the inborn needs of their animals, than modern CEO's * about the innate needs of people.

* and facilities managers, architects, HR-managers, property developers etc.

Four brainchains united:
e-mail and social media are
WEAPONS OF MASS DISTRACTION

After reading the pages above, you will certainly have realized that e-mail, social media, online news etc. are a strong combination of these four BrainChains together. When you are very involved with them, you are

1. Always Being Connected

2. Multitasking

3. Increasing your negative stress

4. Staying up too late

Some people call this the 'e-mail monster'. But it isn't a monster at all, because you create it yourself. It is your very own email Frankenstein. If you don't learn to control your Frankenstein, it will destroy your intellectual productivity, creativity and wellbeing. I will explain further on how you can tame your Frankenstein.

These are real Weapons Of Mass Distraction, if you let them interfere with your brainwork. For managers, it's worse, because it keeps them away from their core-job: being involved with people. I explained before why these Weapons Of Mass Distraction are so addictive, not to discourage you, but to make you aware that getting back in control might be very difficult. If you are forewarned, then you can prepare yourself.

In the beginning, breaking the habit is tough. If you are addicted, you will find dozen reasons why not to change. Once you have developed new habits it becomes much easier to resist, although, you might fall back into the old bad habits occasionally. Everyone does. Even I do.

WEAPONS OF MASS DISTRACTION

DESTROYING INTELLECTUAL PRODUCTIVITY

Worldwide, in 2016
We sent 204 million emails
and 20.8 million WhatsApp's.
We did 4 million Google searches.
We shared 3 million Facebook snippets
We viewed 2.8 million YouTube videos
and 1 million Vine videos.
We assessed 1 million Tinder partners
We shared 527,000 photos on Snapchat
We sent 50,000 tweets
We spent $183,000 on Amazon.com ...
every single minute!

BRAIN-KILLER: Using your phone or other ICT while driving

Every year there are three times the number of people killed in a car crash with the driver on the phone than were killed on 9/11.

When you drive a car your reflex-brain takes care of the routine. You are so used to this that you think that in the meantime your thinking brain can concentrate on a phone conversation. The hundreds of research projects that I summarized in my book "BrainChains" show that this idea is utterly wrong. Using ICT in the car is the worst cause of distracted driving, because your phone is always there. **It increases the risk of having an accident eightfold and hands-free calling does not make any difference,** because it is your brain that is the bottleneck. Hence, even voice-commands do NOT decrease the risk.

Worse of all: texting while driving increases the risk of an accident 23-fold! Multitasking in the office is bad enough, but usually not dangerous; doing it while driving is. Being on the phone greatly hinders your reaction time. It also affects your vision. It blinds you and creates tunnel vision. It degrades the quality of your phone conversation. Drivers on the phone make 70% more mistakes on primary school level questions. And so, doing business while driving is not only dangerous, it's also bad for business.

Most people think they can do this safely because their attention is so impaired that they no longer realize just how screwed up it is. They are even blind to the continuous feedback about how badly they drive.

Phone and driving: risk of accident x 4 à 8
TEXTING WHILE DRIVING: RISK X 23

HANDS-FREE and VOICE-COMMANDED
MAKE NO DIFFERENCE
It's your brain that's the bottleneck!

Five BrainChain-Breakers

BRAINCHAIN-BREAKER 1: DISCONNECT frequently

Disconnecting is the crucial success factor

The single most important solution to get the most out of your brain and your ICT is to plan regular slots of disconnected time for uninterrupted, focused work or conversations. If you can't do that, you will never get the best results, because you won't be able to execute the most phenomenal of all solutions: batch-processing (see further on).

The minimum time you should be disconnected is twice a day for 45 minutes each. Fight for it tooth and nail. *You may forget every single piece of advice in this book, but if you implement just this one, it will significantly improve your intellectual productivity.* You will have to be creative, relentless and even ruthless about this, towards your environment and towards yourself.

First, find out what time of the day your thinking brain works best. When I ask this question to people or teams I coach, many don't even know because they let themselves be disturbed at every hour, if not every minute, of the day. If you don't know, start experimenting with timeslots of protected brain-time at different times of the day to find out what works best for you.

For most people the best hours are in the morning after a good night's sleep. Later, I will explain why it is important to schedule this time before you open your emails or any other source of messages. Whatever your best brain-time is, declare it sacred space during to do your most important brainwork and don't let anything disturb you. Safeguard this time like a precious treasure. Don't let anybody steal it from you.

11 REASONS to Disconnect Regularly

1. Disconnect to focus! AbC creates continuous interruptions, kills focus, slows you down, increases errors and compromises safety.

2. Disconnect to reflect: to think far, wide, deep and innovatively!

3. Disconnect to archive, to improve your memory.

4. Disconnect to be creative! Give your archiving brain a chance to find creative combinations of information.

5. Disconnect to be proactive, AbC turns you into continuously reactive and primitive "adhocrats".

6. Disconnect to defeat the information diarrhea! AbC causes information overload.

7. Disconnect to be wise! AbC exhausts your willpower and self-control, it causes decision fatigue.

8. Disconnect to reconnect! AbC often ruins real conversations, discussions and meetings.

9. Disconnect and disengage to think strategically! AbC leads to a fragmented grasshopper view instead of a comprehensive strategic one.

10. Let them disconnect, make them disconnect! Expecting colleagues and employees to AbC is an enormously costly and counterproductive blunder.

11. Get help to disconnect if your connectivity is a bad habit or an addiction.

Disconnect to think strategically

BRAINCHAIN-BREAKER 2: BATCH-TASKING

Start with planning reflection batches

The solution is very simple: to become more efficient and intellectually productive and have less stress, you must radically and ruthlessly reduce the number of task-switches.

The solution is batch-tasking or batch-processing. This means that first you organize an ironclad donot-disturb cage around your important brainwork. Continuously checking your e-mail and social media is the worst enemy of your thinking brain. The other deadly enemy is an open plan office layout.

Ruthlessly organize your working environment to eliminate distractions. If you have a door, close it. If you don't have a door, look for a space that has one or put a screen around your workspace, put earplugs in your ears and a big headphone on your head, it doesn't even have to work, but it functions as a strong "do not disturb" message. Put up a "do not disturb" sign, switch-off your phone and all the popup screens and beeps on your computer. Put a clever do-not disturb message on your voicemail and out of office email. Finish it off with a break for archiving the information you just processed. The more difficult the work you did, the longer the break should be.

This is the most important advice of this whole book. To be productive and creative, you have to protect your fantastic but vulnerable and easily tired thinking-brain against all the endless distractions that hijack your primitive, tough and tireless reflexbrain.

RIGHT-tasking = BATCH-TASKING
Reflection Batches

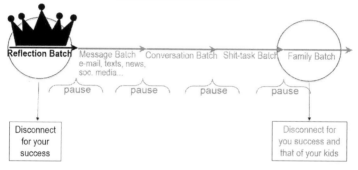

The most difficult batch: putting all Weapons Of Mass Distraction in MESSAGE BATCHES

If you ever want to restore the full power of your thinking brain, you have to be in control of your ICT instead of the other way around. You have to break the very counterproductive habit of looking at your phone all the time and do it radically. You have no choice.

This the most crucial action you can take to liberate your brainpower. Period.

You should handle your emails, messages, social media and news in as few batches per day as possible. For most people this is four batches per day. You must put an impenetrable wall around this batch. You should manage these batches with the attitude of a real professional, not as an addicted consumer. YOU ought to decide how much time you will spend on them, where you do it and when. You should do this batch in a professional environment with professional hardware and software, NOT on your smartphone with two clumsy thumbs on a Tom Thumb screen. Your phone is a gadget and an emergency tool. It's totally unfit for efficient professional work.

You will be astonished how much less time you will spend on your emails and how much better they will be, if you do them in batches and then stop connecting the rest of the day. This is very difficult in the beginning, but once you get used to it, it makes a huge difference for your productivity, creativity and stress.

So many people who did accomplish noted their increased efficiency with a very surprised "I have so much more time now".

RIGHT-tasking = BATCH-TASKING
Message Batches

Reflection Batch | **Message Batch** e-mail, texts, news, soc. media... | Conversation Batch | Shit-task Batch | Family Batch

WEAPONS OF MASS DISTRACTION

pause — pause — pause — pause

Disconnect for your success

Disconnect for you success and that of your kids

A FEW TIPS to bring PEACE to your thinking brain

Unlearn the inefficient habit of answering emails immediately. Every professional has the right and the obligation to do uninterrupted brainwork.

Do important thinking work in the morning and postpone emails and messages until you finished that batch.

Eliminate all sirens that lure you to your inbox, where the ship of your creativity will strand: eliminate all beeps and pop up screens. They should not decide when you look at messages, you should. Unsubscribe from all the automatic messages from the big time-wasters of email, social media and news.

Learn how simple it is to make your e-mail program file CC-mails automatically.

Don't use your inbox as a to-do list but put important work at once in your agenda and unim-

portant chores on a list for your shit-task-batch. (see next)

If you are afraid of totally disconnecting to protect important brainwork, because you fear missing something really urgent organize an emergency escape. Ask a colleague to keep an eye on your phone and emails to warn you when you get a really urgent request. Get a small private emergency phone that's always on and mention its number in your out of office email and voicemail, only for people who really do need you urgently.

In my book "BrainChains" you will find many more very detailed, practical and time-tested tips and tricks.

Don't let unplanned CHATS AND SHIT-TASKS ruin your important brainwork, and batch-task at home too

Shit-tasks are little tasks you don't like, and can't delegate. You are frustrated when you get them and you try to postpone them but they keep nagging at you from the back of your mind. Way too often you have to set aside much more important work, because suddenly a little shit-task became urgent.

The solution is to plan a shit-task-batch every week. Then, when you get a shit-task you can put it on a list and schedule a time slot once a week to handle them all. If you do that, you get less frustrated when you receive one and it won't keep nagging at you because you planned a time to handle it. Hence, there is less risk they will disturb important work. Moreover, doing one of these tasks does not give you much satisfaction, but when you clean up a heap of them, especially just before the weekend, it gives you a feeling of satisfaction.

Last, but not least, you should do batch-tasks at home too. Organize connection free time for work, homework, and connecting with each other. This is especially important if you have children. To my surprise, my research showed that children who are always connected and multitasking from a young age do not handle their ICT better. Not only are the "digital natives" not digital savvy, but always being connected has a negative influence on many aspects of their development. They too have to learn to batchtask and they should learn this as young as possible. The best place to acquire this career saving skill is at home and in school.

RIGHT-tasking = BATCH-TASKING
Important Batches

Reflection Batch | Message Batch — e-mail, texts, news, soc media.. | Conversation Batch | Shit-task Batch | Family Batch

pause   pause   pause   pause

Disconnect for your success

Disconnect for you success and that of your kids

BRAINCHAIN-BREAKER 3: 6 ways to keep your STRESS IN BALANCE

The image of a stress-balance expresses that your goal is to find a balance for every level of demand you might have: there are always six possible solutions.

1. You can decrease the demands. If you have too much on your plate it's usually because you do not say "No", or "Yes if..." when you should. Being always connected weighs heavy on this scale.

2. You can increase your resources, summarized in the acronym **R-TEAM**: Are you taking good care of yourself, your **Resilience,** your fitness? Do you manage your **Time** well? The massive time-waster is always being connected and the ensuing multitasking. Do you have the **Expertise** to cope with the demands; if not, should you get schooling or training? When you cope with the demands, do you give full **Attention** or are you continuously distracted? Finally, do you have the **Material** means, the hardware, software, people and money needed to succeed.

3. Your stress-balance is a subjective one. Are you aware that your interpretation of the situations may cause the imbalance? If you can't change it, look for a coach or therapist trained in cognitive psychology.

4. Do you sufficiently invest in your social support system, the most important resilience-increasing factor?

5. Do you carefully manage your area of control so that you never lose the feeling of having an influence on your balance?

6. Do you get sufficient breaks and sleep? See below.

YOUR STRESS BALANCE

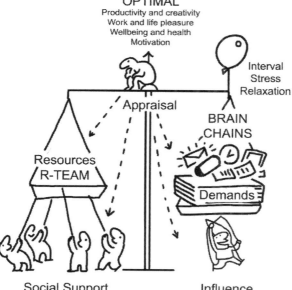

OPTIMAL
Productivity and creativity
Work and life pleasure
Wellbeing and health
Motivation

Interval
Stress
Relaxation

Appraisal

BRAIN
CHAINS

Resources
R-TEAM

Demands

Social Support

Influence

To better MANAGE STRESS use your pause button

When you experience signals that your stressbalance is out of equilibrium, I have one potentially lifesaving advice: push your pause button. With this I do not mean take a long weekend off or go on a vacation. You only have to develop the habit of taking a one minute break. There is never an excuse not to do this. You can do this behind your desk, in the elevator, even in the middle of a meeting.

In this one minute, you think about the two graphs I presented in the chapters about stress

Reflecting on the one explaining how our performance varies with the demands on us, you figure out where you are on that graph. From your position on the slope, you can conclude **how urgent** it is to restore the balance. Then, you think about the figure of the stress-balance and the six areas where you can intervene to restore your balance to decide **what you are going to do**.

Sometimes there is an immediate solution like taking a longer break immediately. Often you may conclude that you need more time to reflect on what's going on and plan the time for this reflection at once. You may conclude that you have been working too many hours and decide to go home soon. You may conclude that things are really getting out of hand and that you are going to take more time to think about it and to have an assertive conversation with your boss, spouse, etc. about what is causing your stress imbalance. More on this in my books "BrainChains" and "Stress: Friend and Foe".

USE THE PAUSE BUTTON!
Only one minute!

BRAINCHAIN-BREAKER 4: Give your brain the PAUSES AND SLEEP it needs to excel

For your archiving-brain to archive, for your thinking brain to recuperate and to restore your stress-balance, you should have a break after every single task that requires thinking, attention and concentration. You should not skip lunch, or continue to work while having lunch. Having a proper lunchbreak, where you disconnect from work, is an excellent investment in the quantity and quality of your brainwork.

Working extra hours does not increase productivity or creativity; on the contrary, it decreases it. Stop the workday in time to allow time to recuperate. Always being connected creates the risk that all boundaries between work and private life disappear. The negative consequences for your brainwork far outweigh the gains. Moreover, it creates unrelenting chronic stress, which is a killer. If you think you really must work on the weekends, carefully batchprocess work at home.

Reorganize your life around the results of the two sleep-tests on the right page. For your biological clock, you should start with getting up every day at the same time. If you need more sleep on the weekends, go to bed earlier. Ideally, you should plan all important, difficult or complex brainwork in the morning after a good night's sleep and before you look at your messages. That way you will get the maximum benefit from the important work your archiving brain did during the time you were asleep to prepare you for the day. You can find many more tips in "BrainChains".

WHAT IS ENOUGH SLEEP FOR YOU

<u>Test 1</u>. The hours of sleep you need so that you don't need to sleep-in in the week-ends

<u>Test 2</u>. The hours of sleep you need to get through the workday feeling rested, lucid and alert <u>without stimulants</u>

(no caffeine, no coffee, no black or green tea, no coke, no energy (*LOL!*) drinks, no amphetamines, cocaine etc...)

-Without symptoms of sleep-debt such as:
difficult getting out of bed, feeling sleepy, feeling tired, nodding off, feeling drowsy while driving!, needing a nap, craving for junk food or sugar after you had a normal meal, sleeping extra hours in weekend

-Without brain symptoms such as:
Concentration↓ Memory ↓ Patience ↓ Feeling for nuance ↓ Insight ↓ Judgement ↓ Creativity ↓ Multitasking ↓ Decision capability ↓ Depression ↑ Moodiness ↑ Happiness ↓ Enthusiasm ↓ Sexual desire ↓

Warning: the first 14 days without caffeine you may have withdrawal symptoms, such as lack of concentration, headaches, feeling feverish, feeling tired.

BRAINCHAIN-BREAKER 5: Take action for BRAIN-FRIENDLY OFFICES

An office is not a cost, but a means a company invests in to optimize intellectual productivity. Their brains are the most important tool of office workers to be optimally productive. Therefore, offices should satisfy the needs of brainworkers and their brains.

To design an office, executives should know the instructions for use of brainworkers and their brains. The first priority of the design should be enabling focus, attention and concentration, NOT communication. Therefore, the elimination of unwanted interruptions, especially noise and particularly other people's phone calls is very important. The second priority is to stimulate communication. There is a simple test: if you can hear other people's phone calls, you work in an office that's inadequate for brainwork that requires concentration.

To stimulate the intellectual productivity in a sustainable way, a modern flexible office has three foundations: 1. Flexible management 2. Flexible and assertive employees. 3. A flexible office space.

The goal is simple: employees should always have the office space available that fits the work they need to do at that moment. There are, in general, four kinds of work to do in an office: Thinking, Communicating, Collaborating and Recuperating. It is crucial that these functions are not combined into one space.

The worst mistake a company can make is to combine tasks that need communicating with tasks that need focused reflection in the same space.

Functions of a flexible office

Function	Tasks	Needs	Facilities
Reflect Concentrate	**Focused individual intellectual work, reflection**	**Sensory Privacy Quiet** (!), light, familiar, personal stuff at hand.	Visual/**acoustical shielded** from all the other activities, windows, easy to personalize
Communicate	Life or virtual communication = joint reflection	No distraction (visual and auditory)	Acoustically (and visually) shielded
Collaborate	Group meetings, discussions, presentations, virtual conferences, brainstorming	Stimulating, room, light,	Space, windows, good acoustics, tools, technology, not disturbing others
Recuperate	Time out: relax and recuperate or be active	Or quiet Or interactive Or active	→"library" →"pantry-lounge" →"physical activity"

Beware ! Don't let other functions ruin reflection !
Don't mix reflection with other functions in the same space

"It's the only place left
that's not open plan!"

LIFESAVING ADVICE: never ever use your phone or other ICT while driving

Since you now know that using a phone while driving is life-threatening multitasking, you may wonder why it's not prohibited by law. In a conversation with civil servants, I learned that politicians are aware of the danger of using a phone while driving but that they do not want to introduce a total ban because there is no public support for it. Since politician's horizon are as far as the next election, they do not want to take away the drivers' favorite toy, even if using it is as dangerous as drunk driving.

Moreover, automotive and ICT companies lobby hard against any such laws because they make a profit through the sale and use of these dangerous devices. If carmakers and ICT companies really cared about your safety more than their profit, they would automatically disable the use of a phone or a dashboard computer as soon as the car started, except for emergency calls. They should keep the navigator as close as possible to the center of your field of vision and impossible to reset while driving.

Hence, while we are waiting for self-driving cars to take over , you will have to take responsibility yourself for not risking the lives of your passengers or yourself!

By the way, using your phone while riding a bike or walking is also not a good idea. Researchers studying the behavior of pedestrians on the phone, call them "Digital Dead Walkers" and "Digital Zombies". From 2005 to 2010, the number of pedestrians injured while on the phone increased by 600%!

DON'T USE YOUR PHONE WHILE DRIVING!

Just Don't.

OUR HOPE FOR THE FUTURE:
teaching KIDS how to use ICT to their advantage

Initially I thought that our hope for the future lies with the new generations of digital natives. The saddest surprise of my research was that most digital natives do not become digitally savvy, but addicted consumers instead. The younger and more often they are involved with screens, the worse they function in all areas, even at multitasking.

This does not mean that schools should throw out ICT, on the contrary they should embrace it. First as an educational tool and second to teach children how to become the masters, instead of the slaves, of their beautiful but addictive technology.

On the one hand, schools can use educational technology to customize teaching to the specific needs of a pupil, to make drill exercises more fun and to make the digital natives digitally savvy, for example by teaching them to program.

On the other hand, children should learn that always being connected and multitasking ruins learning. Educators should warn them that that technology companies are trying to make them addicted to their screens, and show them how they can avoid these consumer traps.

From very early on they should learn the most important solution: to keep learning and consuming separated by continuously applying and exercising batch-tasking. Most important for their success and wellbeing is knowing how to protect the study/learning batches against all interruptions from social media.

Physical reality of your child

Cognitive reality of your child

Conclusion

The fundamental
SCIENTIFIC FACTS are simple

1. Your thinking brain cannot multitask; it can only manage one task at a time.

2. When you try to multitask, your thinking brain has to switch continuously between tasks.

3. Each switch, even if you are only distracted by the tiniest disruption, lowers your concentration, attention, memory, efficiency and productivity.

4. Your conscious, slow, easily tiring, fragile yet sophisticated, human reflecting-brain needs to be managed well, otherwise your unconscious, fast, untiring and robust, but primitive and bestial reflexbrain will make too many wrong decisions on important matters.

5. Your archiving-brain competes with your reflecting-brain for the same "processor time" and therefore it needs ample breaks and sleep.

6. Always being connected causes low, but chronic unrelenting background stress.

7. Negative stress, even at a low level when it's chronic, undermines the best achievements of your thinking brain: abstract thinking, logical thinking, analytical thinking, creative thinking, empathic thinking and synthetic thinking etc. It also causes local problems such as muscle and joint pain and undermines your physical abilities and health.

8. Using any kind of ICT while driving increases the risk of an accident by 8 to 23 times.

9. Most open offices are brainwork-hostile and have a detrimental impact on intellectual productivity and health.

Three brains influence our thinking and doing

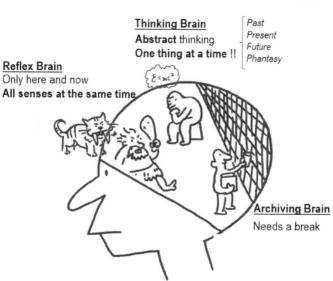

Thinking Brain
Abstract thinking
One thing at a time !!

Past
Present
Future
Phantasy

Reflex Brain
Only here and now
All senses at the same time

$\mathcal{E} = mc^2$

Archiving Brain
Needs a break

The most IMPORTANT SOLUTIONS are simple, but not always easy to apply

1. Don't multitask but batch-task: radically and ruthlessly eradicate as many switches as possible.

    a. Batch-process work that needs reflection

    b. Batch-process emails and other messages

    c. Batch process meetings

    d. Batch-process shit-tasks

    e. Batch process at home

Handle your batches as a professional with professional tools, not with a smartphone or tablet. Pause after every batch to archive and recuperate

2. Disconnect to Think: eliminate all possible distractions and interruptions.

3. Disconnect to have regular breaks: mini-breaks, long breaks and sufficient sleep.

    a. For your thinking brain to recuperate and to be strong enough to rein in your untiring reflex brain.

    b. For your archiving brain to file the zillions of bits of information and to find the information your thinking brain needs to make good, well considered, creative and wise decisions.

    c. For your whole body, to relax and recuperate. Remember: healthy stress is interval stress.

4. Save a life, maybe your own, by NEVER EVER using your phone or other ICT while driving.

5. Avoid doing any brainwork, except routine work, in open offices: collaborate, conspire or revolt to get flexible offices where focus is the first priority.

THE THREE COMMANDMENTS

Rule nr 1

Ruthlessly, radically, eradicate switches BATCH-TASK !

Rule nr 2

Disconnect to reflect

Rule nr 3

Disconnect for a break

To save a life, maybe your own
NEVER EVER use ICT while driving!

Further reading

"**BRAINCHAINS.** Discover your brain and unleash its full potential in a hyperconnected multitasking world" **www.brainchains.info**

"**The Open Office Is Naked**" **www.brainchains.info** Tab "Free book"

"**Stress: Friend and Foe**" **www.compernolle.com** Tab "Books and Tools"

For e-book versions of these books: **www.smashwords.com**

References

You can find the hundreds of references to the research publications on which this book is based in "BRAINCHAINS" or in a list you can download free at www.brainchains. info Tab "Free texts"

Comments, feedback and questions

Please send your feedback, comments, edits or questions to comments@brainchains.info

More feedback from readers of BrainChains

It is amazing (and disturbing) that what Theo writes of is so little known and/or poorly embraced by the business world. ... Yet the working practices encouraged by firms, and societies as a whole serve to squander our IQ, EQ and SQ and foster burnout, unrealised potential and underperformance.....And the hyperconnectivity of recent years brought about by the smartphone has magnified the problem multiplefold. Congratulations to Theo for bringing this issue into the open with such a well-evidenced, thoughtful and readable analysis.

L. Watson

Excellent Book. I was addicted to "multitasking" and had trouble concentrating in longer tasks... Can honestly say that this book has changed me for the better!

It is written in a very readable fashion and contains practical tips on how to make you brain work better and more efficiently. It's a kind of "User manual to your brain". How to use it correctly to gain the most stress free productivity...

Jose Rivero

Being filled all the time by all kinds of electronic information every day, I often feel myself lost in this "ICT world". How can we live and what shall we live as human? This book shows me a so powerful human brain ... Looking inside into my brain, I get my idea to have my life back under my own control, just like what is said in the last poem: Recapture time to love and be loved, it is the keystone of happiness and resilience: yours and theirs.

Wei TAO, Business Information Manager

Wow. 6/12 into purchase of this book is still being pulled on and off my shelf. An amazing insight into our brain- possibly the best computer we will ever have the pleasure of owning! I've Learned lots already from this entertaining academic. Enlightening.

S.A.W. Bristol UK

Brilliant book and explodes all the rubbishy myths about multitasking

10HS

... blending his best knowledge in medical sciences and leadership development to give us a real eye opener on how our brain is working (or not) in our new environment.

Serge Zimmerlin. Group Vice President

The book was a revelation for me and helped me better understand why people do what they do in a health & safety context. An essential and easy read for practical people, who want to know how people work and what can be practically done to maximize their efficiency and reduce human error"

Malc Staves Global Health & Safety Director

... Innovations that work are selected and thrive, but some, like IT and hyperconnectedness, overshoot and threaten to become runaway phenomena. It took Prof. Compernolle's unique synthesis of brain science, expertise in human behavior and therapeutical skills to also provide remedies and to progress from Drucker's 'knowledge work' to Compernolle's 'brainwork'.

Prof. Jan Bernheim

A MUST READ for managers overall, but especially for responsible HR managers as the productivity of esp. white-collar employees is truly at risk in the 'Anytime, Anyplace' connected world of today. The research and in-practice evidence is overwhelming why we should not multitask, always be connected or take short cuts on our sleep. I compare the impact of this book to the "Shallows: what the internet does to our brains" by N.Carr.

I have changed my personal habits immediately and now also inspire people around me at work and in my private life to do the same.

Philippe

It's obvious that our best tool to work and live it's our brain but unfortunately we often forget the way to use it correctly. Theo, in the funniest way I know, has found the right way to open my mind and improve my daily performance. Reading this book you will know how many mistakes make every day avoiding to use our brain correctly and how much time/money we could save hearing our body signals.

Ferdinand

"...Multitasking is impossible! Understanding and accepting this, helped me to refocus on tasks which matters and to rediscover my creativity. I used the short MULTITASKING test in my meetings in our global organization. It's exciting to see everywhere the "aha"-effect, the epiphany!"

Dr. Peter zum Hebel, Vice President

An absolute must if we want to safeguard or recover our brain's full capacity, productivity and creativity. A wise lesson to better master the ever growing number of addictive ICT-tools, thus improving our quality of life both at home and at work, and, who knows, even saving lives.

And finally, a plea for more direct and true relationships in the real world instead of losing precious time in a mostly shallow virtual world

Prof Gino Baron

This book provides a number of important data that caution us to ask ourselves important questions about our habits and how we ruin our companies, families, health and safety by blindly following manufacturers of various gadgets. Highly recommended!

Vedran Vucic

Your Notes:

Printed in Great Britain
by Amazon